NORTH

Learn Everything You Need To Know About North Korea During The USA & North Korean Missile Conflict – IN LESS THAN 30 MINUTES

Jay Benright

Table of Contents

North Korea - Introduction

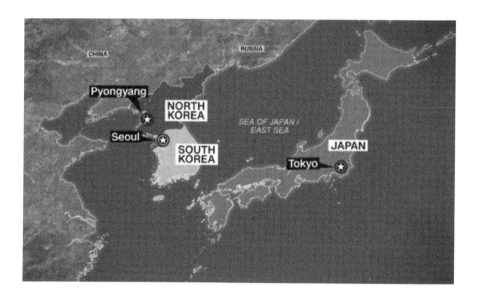

Introduction

North Korea might be the most unusual country of any country on the globe at this moment in time. No other country has isolated their citizens as effectively from influences of the entire world as the North Korean Government has done to its people. The North Korean Government built a quite effective wall like border around their country that not only keep their citizens inside – they have effectively used their "Wall" to keep others outside from entering their country.

This "Wall" extends to the Media and Internet as well. Virtually all 25 million North Korean Citizens have no access to any outside media or Internet. All media broadcast stations are controlled by the Government. The North Korean Government keeps their citizens isolated and under firm control by controlling the information that each citizen is allowed to see, hear & read.

The result of this economic and information isolation is a country whose citizens have one of the hardest day-to-day living conditions on the planet. For many of its citizens it's just about surviving until the next day. Furthermore because of their isolation - on a social and behavioral level the citizens of North Korea have many unique behaviors and beliefs that are found in no other country. We will discuss many of these unique behaviors along with some unusual beliefs.

In this book we explore North Korea, it people and the current missile conflict between North Korea and the USA & South Korea. The goal with this book is to give you a very solid understanding of North Korea is a very short period of time. With all this escalation of talk of military conflict even on a nuclear level, its important that everyone understand the country of North Korea, the threat to the world that it imposes and just what are the stakes involved.

Chapter 1 – History, Government & People

History

An independent kingdom for much of its long history, Korea was occupied by Japan beginning in 1905 following the Russo-Japanese War. In 1910, Japan formally annexed the entire peninsula. Following World War II in 1945, Korea was split with the northern half coming under Soviet-sponsored communist control while the South was aligned with regional and worldwide democracies.

In 1950, North & South Korea went to war. The United States supported South Korea with both arms and troops. China & Russia supported North Korea with the same. The fighting was brutal; as many accounts have talked of even hand-to-hand combat in frozen conditions after soldiers ran out of ammunition. While there is no universal agreement as to the total number of people who died in the war the best estimates are over a million people at least. USA Military Deaths were around 36,000 with a significant larger number wounded.

After failing in the Korean War (1950-53) to conquer the US-backed Republic of Korea (ROK) in the southern portion by force, North Korea, under its founder President KIM Il-Sung, adopted a policy of ostensible diplomatic and economic "self-reliance" as a check against outside influence.

Since the end of the Korea war, North Korea has consistently told its citizens that the USA is the ultimate threat to its social system through state-funded media, and molded political, economic, and military policies around the core ideological objective of eventual unification of Korea under Pyongyang's – the capital of North Korea - control.

KIM Il-Sung's son, KIM Jong-il, was officially designated as his father's successor in 1980, assuming a growing political and managerial role until the elder KIM's death in 1994. His son - KIM Jong-Un was publicly unveiled as his father's successor in 2010. It was under his reign that the Korean leader started to take on a mythical god like persona to the Korean people as we discuss later.

Following KIM Jong-il's death in 2011, his son KIM Jong-Un quickly assumed power and has now taken on most of his father's former titles and duties.

Since the mid-1990s North Korea has faced chronic food shortages. In recent years, the North's domestic agricultural production has increased, but it still falls far short of producing sufficient food to provide for its entire population. North Korea began to ease restrictions to allow semi-private markets, starting in 2002, but has made few other efforts to meet its goal of improving the overall standard of living.

North Korea's history of regional military provocations; proliferation of military-related items; long-range missile development; WMD programs including tests of nuclear devices in 2006, 2009, 2013, and 2016; and massive conventional armed forces are of major concern to the international community and have limited the DPRK's international engagement, particularly economically. The regime abides by a policy calling for the simultaneous development of its nuclear weapons program and its economy.

Geography

North Korea land size is close to the size of the state of Pennsylvania. The terrain consists of mostly hills and mountains separated by deep and narrow valleys. The west has wide coastal plains. 22% of the North Korea is devoted to agriculture, forests cover 46%.

Climate & Weather
Temperate with rainfall mostly in the summer. However winters are seasonally long and very cold.

Population
The Population of North Korea is estimated to be a 25.1 million people making North Korea the 51st largest country. The population is concentrated in the plains and lowlands of the country. The least populated regions are the mountainous provinces adjacent to the Chinese border. The largest concentrations are in the western provinces, particularly the municipal district of its capital Pyongyang, and around Hungnam and Wonsan in the east. The one common language is Korean.

Life expectancy at Birth is 70.4 years. For men the life expectancy is 66.6 years. For women the life expectancy is 74.7. Korea ranks 157 in the world for life expectancy.

North Korea has one of the worlds lowest obesity rate – only 2.5% of the adult population is obese – compared to 38% in the USA. However the low obesity rate is probably attributable to shortages of food more so than healthy lifestyles.

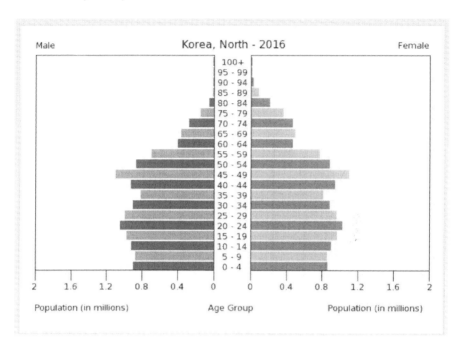

North Korea claims to have one of the worlds highest Literacy rates as nearly 100% of the adult population can read and write.

Religion
North Korea's traditional religions were Buddhist and Confucianism, some Christian and syncretic Chondogyo (Religion of the Heavenly Way). Independent religious activities are now almost nonexistent. Government-sponsored religious groups exist to provide illusion of religious freedom

Government
North Korea is a communist state. There are nine governing provinces and two special ruling cities.

The nine provinces are Chagang, Hambuk (North Hamgyong), Hamnam (South Hamgyong), Hwangbuk (North Hwanghae), Hwangnam (South Hwanghae), Kangwon, P'yongbuk (North Pyongan), P'yongnam (South Pyongan), Ranggang

The 2 ruling cities are Pyongyang, Rason - Rason is sometimes designated as a special city and Pyongyang is the capital city where the President - currently Kim Jong-Un – lives and governs from.

President
The President is Kim Jong-Un. He was born January 8, 1984 which makes him 33 year old today.

Kim Jong-Un was declared supreme leader of North Korea on December 28, 2011 after the funeral of his farther Kim Jong-il – who was the supreme ruler of North Korea from 1994-2011. Kim Jong-Un grandfather - Kim Il-Sung – was the supreme leader of North Korea from its founding in 1948 to his death in 1994.

Constitution
The North Korean Constitution was created in 1948 modified in 1972. The constitution has been revised in 2009, 2012, 2013 (2016)

Executive Branch of Government

Chief of State - Supreme ruler is Kim Jong-Un (since December 2011)

Premier - PAK Pong Ju (since 2 April 2013);

Vice Premiers - 8
Jon Kwant Ho since January 17, 2017
RI Ju O since June 29, 2016)
RI Ryong Nam since June 29, 2016
KO In Ho since June 29, 2016
IM Chol Ung since May 29, 2014
KIM Tok Hun since June 19, 2013
RI Mu Yong since 31 May 31, 2011
RO Tu Chol since September 3, 2003

Cabinet - Cabinet or Naegak members are appointed by the Supreme People's Assembly except for the Minister of People's Armed Forces

Executive Elections & Appointments – The Chief of State and premier are indirectly elected by the Supreme People's Assembly. The election was last held on March 9, 2014. The election results were KIM Jong-Un was reelected as he ran unopposed

The Korean Workers' Party continues to list deceased leaders KIM Il-Sung and KIM Jong-il - Kim Jong-Un Father & Grandfather - as Eternal President and Eternal General Secretary respectively

Legislative Branch of Government

Called the unicameral Supreme People's Assembly or Ch'oego Inmin Hoeui - 687 seats whose members directly are elected by absolute majority vote to serve 5-year terms. It should be noted that the Korean Workers' Party (KWP) selects all the candidates.

The elections were last held on March 9, 2014. The next election is scheduled to be held in March 2019. The ruling party approves a list of candidates who are elected without opposition; a token number of seats are reserved for minor parties

Judicial Branch of Government

Highest court(s): Supreme Court or Central Court which consists of the chief justice and two "People's Assessors" and for some cases 3 judges. The Supreme People's Assembly elects the judges for 5-year terms.

Subordinate courts consist of provincial, municipal, military, special courts; people' courts (lowest level)

Political Parties

The Major party is the Korean Workers' Party or KWP. Kim Jong-Un is leader of this party.
Minor parties: Chondoist Chongu Party - this party is under KWP control.
Social Democratic Party, KIM Yong Dae — this party is also under KQWP control (under KWP control)

Korean Flag

The Korean Flag consist of three horizontal bands of blue (top), red (triple width), and blue. The red band is edged in white. On the hoist side of the red band is a white disk with a red five-pointed star; the broad red band symbolizes revolutionary traditions, the narrow white bands stand for purity, strength, and dignity. The blue bands signify sovereignty, peace, and friendship; the red star represents socialism

Chapter 2 – Economy & Military

Economy

North Korea is one of the world's most centrally directed and least open economies. North Korea has always faced chronic economic problems throughout its entire existence. Industrial manufacturing facilities are nearly beyond repair as a result of years of underinvestment, shortages of spare parts, and poor maintenance. There have been repeated food shortages throughout the country's history. The Country is poor in energy and other natural resources.

Large-scale military spending and development of its ballistic missile and nuclear program severely drains resources needed for investment and civilian consumption. Industrial and power outputs have stagnated for years at a fraction of pre-1990 levels. Frequent weather-related crop failures aggravated chronic food shortages caused by on-going systemic problems, including a lack of arable land, collective farming practices, poor soil quality, insufficient fertilization, and persistent shortages of tractors and fuel.

The mid 1990s were marked by severe famine and widespread starvation. The international community through 2009 provided significant food aid. Since that time, food assistance has declined significantly. In the last few years, domestic corn and rice production has improved, although domestic production does not fully satisfy demand. A large portion of the population continues to suffer from prolonged malnutrition and poor living conditions.

Since 2002, the government has allowed semi-private markets to begin selling a wider range of goods, allowing North Koreans to partially make up for diminished public distribution system rations. It also implemented changes in the management process of communal farms in an effort to boost agricultural output.

In December 2009, North Korea introduced a new currency, capping the amount of North Korean won that could be exchanged for the new notes and limiting the exchange to a one-week window. A concurrent crackdown on markets and foreign currency use yielded severe shortages and inflation, forcing Pyongyang to ease the restrictions by February 2010.

The North Korean Government continues to stress its goal of improving the overall standard of living, but has taken few steps to make that goal a reality for its citizens. In 2016, the regime used two mass mobilizations — one totaling 70 days and another 200 days — to spur the population to increase production and complete construction projects quickly. The regime released a five-year economic development strategy in May 2016 that outlined plans for promoting growth across sectors. However the structure of centralized control government will likely inhibit formal changes to North Korea's current economic system.

North Korea Annual GDP is estimated to be at around $40 Billion annually. For comparison purposes, Amazon.com had $38 Billion in sales in its most recent 3-month period of time.

North Korea has a labor force of 14 Million people. 37% of the population works in agriculture.

North Korean exports mostly commodity products such as minerals, metallurgical products, manufactures (including armaments), textiles, agricultural and fishery products. North Korea major economic and trading partner is China as 76% of North Korea's exports are to China – almost all of them commodities.

ENERGY
Out of a population of around 25 Million, **18.4 million are living without electricity**. Only 41% of people living in urban areas and only 13% of people in rural areas have electricity.

North Korea has zero oil reserves and imports 100% of their oil, which is around 70,000 barrels a day.

North Korea does not have any Nuclear power plants. Also there is no energy from natural gas with the country having zero proven gas reserves.

Telephone and Cellular Communications
Only 1.2 million people have a fixed line telephone. That works out to 5 per 100 people.

Only 3.3 million people have a cellular telephone. That works out to 13 per 100 people.

Broadcast Media
There is no independent media - **radios and TVs are pre-tuned to government stations**. There are 4 government-owned TV stations; the Korean Workers' Party owns and operates the Korean Central Broadcasting Station, and the state-run Voice of Korea operates an external broadcast service. The government prohibits listening to and jams foreign broadcasts.

Military
North Korea has an Army, Navy, Air Force and civilian security force.

North Korea has the worlds 4th largest military with 1.2 million active duty soldiers and another 600,000 reserves. There are 6.5 million more males available for service and also 6.4 million women available for active service. More than half of North Korean population is either in the Military or available for service.

Both Men and Women have mandatory military service at 17. The term of service for men is 10 years. For Women the term of service is until the age 23.

The border between North Korea and South Korea is the most militarized in the world, according to the State Department. Pyongyang has about 1.2 million military personnel stationed near the border compared with 680,000 troops in South Korea along with 28,000 U.S. troops are also stationed there. Nearly 6 million North Koreans are reservists in the worker/peasant guard, compulsory to the age of 60.

The next photo illustrates the current military strength and capabilities of both North Korea and South Korea. The technological advantage is firmly on the South Korea/USA side. However the North Korean army is large enough and has enough military equipment to cause significant damage and loss of life to the citizens of South Korea in any armed conflict – regardless of who attacked whom first.

Korean military balance Strengths compared

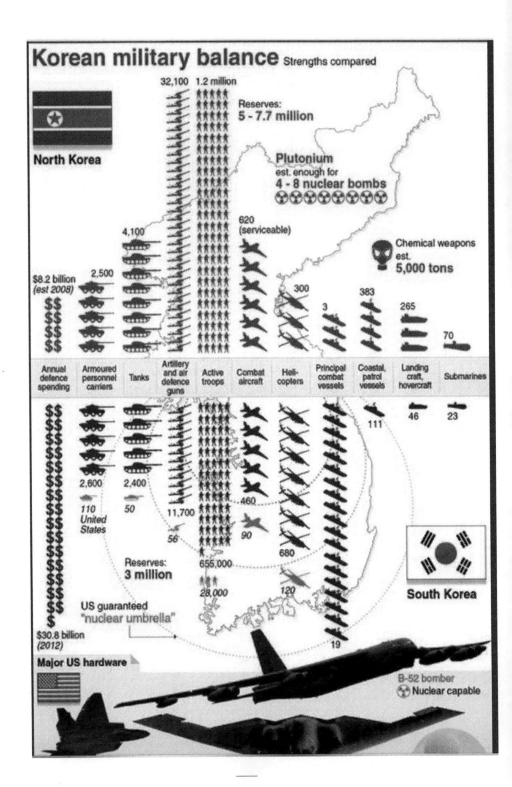

North Korea

| 32,100 | 1.2 million |

Reserves: **5 - 7.7 million**

Plutonium est. enough for **4 - 8 nuclear bombs**

4,100

620 (serviceable)

Chemical weapons est. **5,000 tons**

| $8.2 billion (est 2008) | 2,500 | | | | | 300 | 3 | 383 | 265 | 70 |

Annual defence spending	Armoured personnel carriers	Tanks	Artillery and air defence guns	Active troops	Combat aircraft	Heli-copters	Principal combat vessels	Coastal, patrol vessels	Landing craft, hovercraft	Submarines
								111	46	23
	2,600	2,400								
	110 United States	50	11,700		460					
			56		90					
					680					

Reserves: **3 million**

655,000

28,000

120

US guaranteed "nuclear umbrella"

19

South Korea

$30.8 billion (2012)

Major US hardware

B-52 bomber
Nuclear capable

Forced Labor Camps

North Korea is notorious world wide for their forced labor camps. North Korea currently operates about 16 labor camps—massive compounds scattered across the mountainous terrain and enclosed by electrified barbed wire fences.

The prison cities are often compared to the Gulag camps of Soviet Russia—forced labor camps in which prisoners are held in brutal working conditions and executed for crimes as petty as stealing a food. Prisoners are usually a mix of defectors, traitors, and ex-politicians who ran afoul of the government.

Between 150,000 and 200,000 North Koreans live in prison camps surrounded by electrified fencing, according to South Korean government estimates and Human Rights Watch. The worst camps are for those who commit political crimes, and offenders can have their entire extended family imprisoned with them. As many as 40% of camp prisoners die from malnutrition while doing mining, logging and agricultural work with rudimentary tools in harsh conditions, according to a 2011 Amnesty International report.

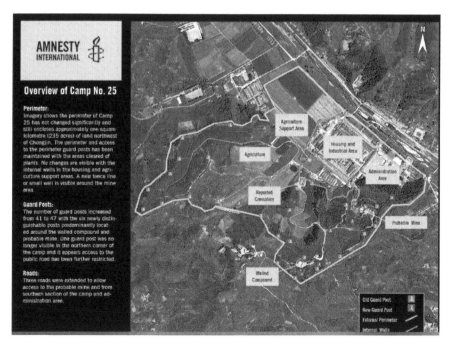

North Korea follows a "three generations of punishment" rule, meaning that if one person violated the law or sent to prison, their children, parents AND grandparents are sent to work with them. Anyone found guilty of committing a crime – such as trying to escape from North Korea to China or South Korea - is sent to the Kaechon internment camp along with his or her entire family. The subsequent two generations would be born IN the camp and must also live their entire lives in servitude and die there.

Between 150,000 and 200,000 North Koreans live in prison camps surrounded by electrified fencing, according to South Korean government estimates and Human Rights Watch. The worst camps are for those who commit political crimes, and offenders can have their entire extended family imprisoned with them. As many as 40% of camp prisoners die from malnutrition while doing mining, logging and agricultural work with rudimentary tools in harsh conditions, according to a 2011 Amnesty International report.

Chapter 3 – Other Interesting & Unusual Facts About North Korea

North Korea's most popular attraction is visiting Kim Jong-il's preserved body. The North Korean dictator's embalmed body rests in a state mausoleum and is open for visitation - even to foreign tourists. The local guides have a comprehensive knowledge of Kim's life and eagerly point out details about his great achievements and godlike abilities.

- In the 50s, North Korea built Kijong-dong, a small city visible from the South Korean Border. The entire city was empty. The purpose was to lure South Koreans in. The city is currently a ghost town today with no permanent residents.

- Risking arrest, imprisonment, and deportation, tens of thousands of North Koreans have crossed into China to escape famine, economic privation, and political oppression.

- Marijuana is legal in North Korea and is not classified as a drug.

- North Korea has 51 "Social Categories" ranked by their loyalty to the Regime.

- North Koreans Men & Women may only choose from 28 approved Hair Styles – Seriously - see the next image:

Approved haircuts in North Korea

- Kim Il-Sung, the founder of North Korea, was born on the day that the Titanic sank.

- Over the past 60 years, 23,000 North Koreans have defected to South Korea. During the last 60 years only 2 South Koreans have defected to the North Korea.

- Being in possession of a Bible, watching South Korean movies or distributing pornography may be punished by death sentence in North Korea.

- Only Military and Government officials may own a motor vehicle.

- Wearing Jeans is Illegal in North Korea.

- According to a textbook in North Korea, President Kim Jong-Un learned to drive a car at age 3.

- North Korea has the world's largest stadium that seats 150,000 people.

- When a single anti Kim Jong-il graffiti was found in Pyongyang, North Korea, the entire city of over 2 million people was locked down for 3 days.

- In 2011 North Korean researchers concluded that North Korea is the second happiest country in the world. China their largest trading partner was the happiest country.

- It is mandatory for North Korean citizens to vote even though there is only one candidate to choose for each office.

- North Koreans born after the Korean War are two inches shorter on average than South Koreans.

- Less than 3% of the roads in North Korea are paved.

- In North Korea, the Internet is limited to a very small circle of the elite (only 1,579 IP addresses exist for a population of 25 million). North Korea also has their own operating system called Red Star and the content is pre-filtered by the state. Red Star is based on Linux and runs a state-approved search engine. Chats, emails, and forum boards are regularly monitored and Internet access in general is only permitted with special authorization and primarily used for government purposes or by foreigners

A night image of the Korean Peninsula taken by NASA illustrates the sheer isolation and underlying electricity problems in North Korea (as mentioned earlier). Compared to its neighbors South Korea and China, it is nearly completely dark. See in the photo for how North Korea looks at night from space.

- North Koreans are told that Kim Jong-Il - who is the Current president Kim Jong-Un Father and former President - was apparently born under a double rainbow and his birth caused a new star to appear in the sky. He learned to walk and talk before 6 months and has the ability to control the weather by his moods. At least that what it says according to the official government-released biography of his life.

- Kim Jong-il, son of the country's founder, has performed amazing feats, according to state-controlled media. He scored a perfect 300 the first time he went bowling and sank 11 holes-in-one the first time he played golf.

- There are an estimated 34,000 statues of Kim Il-Sung in North Korea — one for every 3.5 kilometer or one statue for every 750 people.

- The founder and first leader of North Korea, Kim Il-Sung, created the country's policy of JUCHE or "self-reliance," which cut off North Korea economically and diplomatically from the rest of the world, even in times of great need, such as famines. As many as 2 million people died as a result of famine in the 1990s caused by erratic government farming policies and flooding, according to the

United Nations. Asia Press reported that a recent return of famine in the farming provinces of North and South Hwanghae has forced some to resort to cannibalism.

- In 2013, North Korea's President Kim Jong-Un killed his uncle by throwing him naked in to a cage with 120 starving dogs.

- Two women who used a deadly nerve agent, according to Malaysian authorities, assassinated Kim Jong-Un's older half-brother, Kim Jong Nam, at the Kuala Lumpur airport in Malaysia on Feb. 13, 2017. The Malaysian government blamed North Korean agents for his murder.

- North Korea's regime gets much of its income by exporting to Japan and elsewhere-counterfeit pharmaceuticals, such as Viagra, narcotics such as methamphetamine; counterfeit cigarettes and fake $100 U.S. bills.

Chapter 4 – North Korean Missile Crises 2017

What is the Issue between North Korea and the USA?
In 2017 North Korea launched for the first time an Intercontinental Ballistic Missile (ICBM). The USA military tracked the missile from where it was launched at a North Korean airfield to the Sea of Japan. The missile spent 37 minutes in flight before it landed in the Sea of Japan.

Hasn't North Korea Test Fired Missiles several times already?
Yes, but what makes this time different is this was the first time that North Korea successfully tested a long range two stages ICBM Missile. This ICBM Missile has a range of up to 3,400 miles that would put Alaska, Hawaii within strike range.

Why is North Korea doing this?

North Korea for years has claimed that the U.S., together with South Korea, is engaged in a hostile campaign aimed at overthrowing the North Korean regime. It calls its nuclear and missile program a deterrent to a U.S. attack.

Is the U.S. in danger of an immediate nuclear attack?

Officials seem to believe the North Koreans have not developed the capability to miniaturize a nuclear warhead, a critical technology for placing one atop an ICBM. United States Government officials are worried about North Korea's steadily improving technical capability and apparent determination to deploy such a weapon rapidly. However in August of 2017, the Washington Post reported that Department of Defense officials had intelligence that seemed to suggest that North Korea had developed nuclear weapons for ICBM missiles like the one launched into the Sea of Japan that could reach parts of the USA mainland.

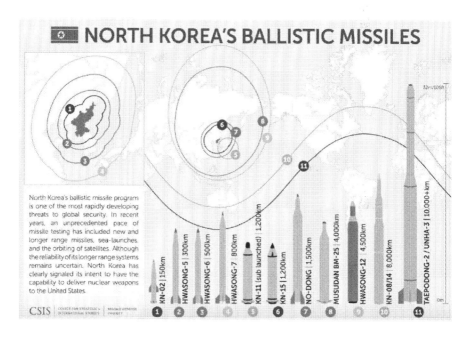

How did the U.S. react to the ICBM Missile Launch?

President Trump condemned the test and asked China to "put a heavy move on North Korea and end this nonsense once and for all!"

President Trump also publicly tweeted a warning that North Korean nuclear threats "will be met with fire, fury and frankly power, the likes of which the world has never seen before". The North Korean Government responded by announcing that it was considering attacking US military bases in the USA Territory of Guam.

At an emergency U.N. Security Council meeting USA ambassador Nikki Haley condemned the ICBM Missile launch by North Korea as "dangerous and irresponsible." She called for even tighter sanctions against trade with North Korea, but warned that the U.S. was prepared to employ a "full range of counter measures" including use of military force if necessary.

What was China's reaction?

Beijing, which is North Korea's largest trading partner and closest ally, has been reluctant to put heavy pressure on North Korea, fearing that an economic collapse of North Korea would create chaos on its own borders. So China suggested a compromise. North Korea would stop missile tests if the United States and South Korea scaled back military exercises in the region. China also looking out for its own interest appreciates the buffer that North Korea provides against the USA and South Korean's. All of the World's superpowers wish to have their immediate geographical neighbors on "their team" and China is not different then the USA & Russia in this regard. China does not wish to wake up and find South Korean & USA military now stationed on its border.

What are the military options for the U.S. and its allies?

A combination of Air bombings, Missile strikes and Naval maneuvers. The USA military would assuredly decimate much of North Korea when fully unleashed. However, the risk of unleashing a larger conflict on the Korean Peninsula would be a near certainty. North Korea has a 1.2-million-member military, and Seoul, the South Korean capital, is just 35 miles from the demilitarized zone marking the border. Conventional weapons from North Korea— including rockets, missiles and artillery — could devastate South Korea even if the U.S. military successfully destroyed North Korea's nuclear sites. Any attack by the USA would leave 25 million South Koreans vulnerable, along with 28,000 U.S. troops stationed there.

How has North Korea responded to the worldwide backlash over its ICBM Test Missile Launch?

North Korea response has been defiance to what the rest of the world thinks. The North Korean Central News Agency said Kim Jong-Un vowed his nation will "demonstrate its mettle to the U.S." and never put its weapons programs up for negotiations. The agency described Kim Jong-Un as "feasting his eyes" on the ICBM and breaking into a "broad smile" while punching the air with his fists to the delight of his generals. He urged his nation's scientists to "frequently send big and small "gift packages to the Yankees," an apparent reference to Kim's intent to push ahead with nuclear and missile tests. Kim Jong-Un also publicly expressed some displeasure with China with some of their proposals for settlement, which is very unusual for North Korea since China is its biggest trading partner and closest ally.

Is there a Good Military Solution Available?

The short answer is no. Under any military option the death toll for both North & South Korea would be in the 100's of thousands at least to the millions of people.

If the USA were to launch a "successful" first strike there is still no chance that the USA military can eliminate all of North Korea's Military capabilities. There are over a million heavily armed soldiers on the Border of South Korea. The city of Seoul South Korea is home to Millions of people. Seoul is well within the range of conventional rockets and missiles that North Korea can launch at any time. Between 1.2 million North Korean soldiers, their Missiles and air force, there is no scenario where many people in South Korea would not die. Guam could also sustain casualties if there was a military conflict.

However, without a doubt the USA military would demolish the North Korean Military in a military conflict. If the USA Government saw the North Korean Army crossing the South Korean Border or if North Korean Launched a military strike against South Korea with missiles as they have threatened the response from the USA military would be severe. In previous conflicts in the Middle East that the USA has engaged in over the past 20 years, many very powerful "conventional" weapons were not used by the USA military because of the outrage that the world would have shown because of their destructive capabilities. However if the USA and South Korea government saw that South Korea was under invasion then the USA military would be forced to use all the conventional weapons in its arsenal and the results would be horrific.

So in any military conflict many people - mostly Korean people in the North & South and American soldiers - will die under the "best of scenarios". Under any scenario, a military conflict will be a suicide mission for North Korea, as they will be destroyed. However as an American, I do wish to see a million or more North Koreans die in an armed conflict that our side would "win". Most of the people in North Korea are Mothers, Fathers, children who are living under severe oppression and are just struggling to survive each day. These people live in constant fear and poverty. Like most people everywhere they want to work, have some enjoyment in life from time to time and have a safe environment to raise their children.

Note that American mainland faces no threat at all now from a conflict with North Korea. As shown by the Image of North Korea at night – this is a country that is to poor and technology challenged to even keep the lights on at night.

So What Should Be Done?
Contrary to what many people think President Trump has done a good job in this crisis. First he has confronted it directly. It should be clear to everyone that North Korea having Nuclear Weapons will make the world a far more dangerous place. Look at some of the examples we have talked about related to what the rulers of North Korea are willing to do to their own people?

Trumps was right on with his initial response was to get China to help with the North Korean Missile crises. China as North Korea only powerful ally along with their largest trading partner is the one with the influence to convince North Korea to abandon its nuclear program. Trump is also right to be directly confronting the North Koreans and the world about stopping North Korea from developing a nuclear weapon instead of ignoring this.

As mentioned there is just not a good Military Solution to this situation. And if the world chooses to ignore the advances that North Korea is making in it both Missiles and nuclear capabilities, then there will be a far larger problem in the future once North Korea has Missiles with the capabilities to deliver a nuclear payload.

About the only feasible option for successfully resolving this situation is for North Korea to be convinced to abandon their nuclear program in exchange for economic development money. World leaders, especially China – should be pushing North Korea to recognize the benefits of opening up its economy like China did 20 years ago. It would take probably a lot of money and resources to sway North Korea to open its economy and abandon its nuclear program. However democratic reforms always follow the opening up of any economy and that would be the best-case scenario for both the North & South Korean people.

Also for the rest of the world would benefit by keeping a major military conflict from breaking out in the near term. What the world cannot tolerate is a future with a government like North Korea that has the nuclear weapons that are capable of destroying 10's of millions of people lives with the push of a button. I see the only path to a successful resolution of this situation is an economic one.

Thanks for purchasing this book. I will update this book from time to time as this crisis unfolds.